ESSENTIAL PARKOUR TRAINING

BASIC PARKOUR STRENGTH AND MOVEMENT

SAM FURY

Illustrated by
RAUL GUAJARDO

WARNINGS AND DISCLAIMERS

CONTENTS

WALL TECHNIQUES

BAR TECHNIQUES

INTRODUCTION

Parkour is one of the most useful ways to get out of immediate danger when on land.

This training manual focuses on essential parkour movements. By "essential," I mean those movements and techniques which, with basic training, would be relatively safe to use without pre-planning—if you were running away from someone in an unfamiliar area, for example.

Why Learn Parkour?

The main reason to learn parkour is the same one for which it was invented: to develop the ability to get from one point to another as efficiently as possible. There are also other benefits, such as:

- It's a fun and challenging way to keep fit. It's exercising without feeling like you're exercising. You just learn the skills; physical fitness is a welcome byproduct.
- It's a good way to socialize with other parkour enthusiasts. Or if you prefer to be a loner, parkour can be practiced solo.
- It lets you see the world around you in a new light. Once you start to learn parkour, you will no longer look at buildings, stairs, rails, or any other structure in the same way again.
- It helps you overcome fear. Many parkour movements, like jumping gaps, can be daunting, but you'll be able to draw on the confidence you gain from succeeding at them in other areas of your life.
- It increases your imagination. Figuring out different ways to get from point to point using parkour skills is good for your creativity.

Progression

Proper progression in parkour is useful for breaking through fear as well as for safety.

Conquer small milestones and gradually increase to bigger goals. After you successfully complete something once, it will get easier. But don't get too cocky. That's how injuries occur.

The techniques in this book are given in a progression according to the type of movement (landing, vault, wall, etc.), but that doesn't mean you need to learn all (or any) of one type of movement before starting to train in another. Almost any type of movement can be practiced at your discretion.

There is one exception: **Proper landing techniques, specifically the safety tap and safety rolling, should be learned first** to prevent injury.

Techniques are presented using the method taught in the Survival Fitness Plan, but there are many ways to learn the same thing. If something doesn't work for you, try it a different way. Adopt the philosophy of using what is good for you and discarding what is not.

Although parkour can be practiced solo, for most people, having a training partner helps with progression, since you will learn from and motivate each other. It's also good for safety.

TRAINING FOR REALITY

Parkour is a great skill to have if you need to run away from an enemy, but training is not the same as having to use it in real life.

Here are some things you can do to prepare yourself in case you need to use parkour in a real-life scenario.

Awareness

Constantly be aware of your surroundings. Use your peripheral vision and formulate a plan of escape whenever you enter a new situation (notice where the exits are, how you would overcome obstacles, etc.).

A side effect of this is that your being aware is obvious. People (would-be attackers) notice that you are, which makes you less of a target.

Outdoors

Train in all terrains, in all types of weather, and in all different types of light.

There are some exceptions. For example, I would not attempt some of the parkour movements on slippery surfaces.

If something is too dangerous to do during training, then it's also too dangerous to do in real life. Remember this if you ever have to make the decision about what to do.

It's also important to vary your training grounds. Training in the same place all the time will limit your imagination, and different situations will require different approaches.

Parkour and Self-Defense

It is highly recommended to combine your parkour training with self-defense. They complement each other very well. For example, the tic-tac can be integrated with a side kick.

Learn more about self-defense training at:

www.SurvivalFitnessPlan.com/Self-Defense-Tutorials

Training on Both Sides

In reality, you should favor the strong side of your body when performing actions. When training, do so on both sides so if you cannot use your strong side (due to an injury, for instance) your weaker side will still be pretty good.

What You Carry

If you habitually carry a bag and are not willing to leave it behind when threatened, then you should train with it on. The tighter the bag fits to your body, the less it will move around when training.

What You Wear

If what you wear in training is not the same thing you wear most of the time, then you won't know if you can execute parkour moves in everyday life. For example, how often do you go out with your climbing shoes on and chalk in your back pocket? If the answer is always, then feel free to use climbing shoes and chalk when training using the Survival Fitness Plan.

Q. So I should train in my suit and tie or skirt and high heels?
A. Yes and no.

Training in clothing that is impractical for physical exercise will hinder your progress, but you should do it at least once in a while so you know what it's like to do parkour in that type of clothing.

You may also want to consider changing what you do wear day to day to ensure functionality in movement. Loose-fitting clothing and sensible shoes can be adapted to almost any situation. Before you put something on, ask yourself, "If I really needed to, would I be able to sprint and climb a wall in this?"

SAFETY

Parkour is not a dangerous activity if you progress slowly, do not take unnecessary risks, and learn the correct safety techniques.

SAFETY TAP

The safety tap is a technique that helps prevent injuries when landing on your feet.

It is good for those times when rolling may not be possible because of a lack of room or other factors, although it's best to use rolls when dropping from greater heights and/or on angles.

To do the safety tap, drop down from a ledge. Start with small drops and work your way up as your confidence builds.

Land on the balls of both feet at the same time, and then roll your heels down towards the ground.

Bend your knees as you land to absorb the shock. Depending on the impact, you can go all the way into a crouch.

Don't slam your wrists down. They are used for assistance and/or balance, but should not be sustaining any major impact.

Spring back up, using the momentum to continue your run.

Try to land as softly and quietly as possible. This is true with most things in parkour. The quieter you are, the softer you are, and the less pressure you put on your joints. Since the practical use for parkour is to run from your enemy, it is also advantageous to be as silent as possible.

When dropping down from a wall (e.g., from a cat hang, for example), it's a good idea to turn away from the obstacle. You may have to use your feet to push away from the wall a little so you can get the room to turn.

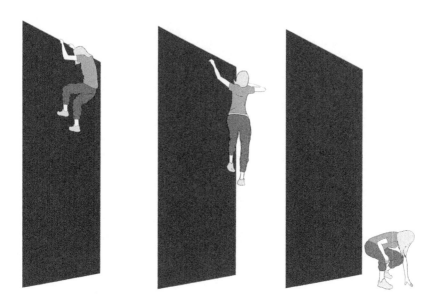

SAFETY ROLLS

The safety roll is an extremely important parkour skill to develop. It is used to prevent injury from a technique gone wrong, a big drop, a general fall or trip, and/or from someone throwing/pushing you to the ground or off something. It's also a good technique for transitioning between movements.

Your aim should be to make your safety roll instinctive. This is because the times you will need it most are those when you are not ready.

The safety roll can be done forwards, sideways, or backwards. You'll probably use the forward roll most often, but you should practice all of them regularly.

When you're first learning the safety roll, do it on soft ground, such as on grass, mats, or sand. Take it slow and start low. Once you have the technique, you can progress by increasing height and/or momentum.

Forward Roll

Choose which side you are most comfortable rolling over, right or left. Eventually, you'll want to learn to roll on both sides.

If rolling over your left shoulder, start from a kneeling position with your left foot forward.

Place your hands on the ground in front of you, so that your thumbs and index fingers form a kind of diamond shape. Put them at a 45° angle in the direction that you want to roll in.

Note: You could just roll over your shoulder, but unless you have something in your hands it's preferable to use them to help control your motion, as well as to absorb some of the impact.

Look over your right shoulder and use your rear leg to push you over into the roll. Use your hands to control your momentum and your arms to lift you a little, so that you can land on the back of your shoulder blade. You do not want to hit on the top of your shoulder.

Roll diagonally across your back to your opposite hip. If you roll wrong (which you probably will when first learning), you'll feel it. When you start practicing on hard surfaces, you will definitely know if you're rolling poorly. It's a learning curve.

Come up from your roll between your tail and hip bones, and use the side of your leg and your momentum to get back onto your feet.

You could also come straight up onto your feet instead of using your thigh. This will save your knee from contacting the ground, but puts more pressure on your ankle as you stand.

As you get more confident, start from taller positions such as squatting and standing. A good exercise is to stand straight and let your body fall forward like a plank.

At the last moment, roll out of it. This can be done with side and back rolls as well.

Progress to rolling with momentum and with jumps. When jumping into a roll, be sure to keep your legs flexed as you land and allow the momentum to push you into the roll.

Eventually you will be able to jump and roll from ledges. It is important to slowly work your way up and increase the strength in your legs so that you can do bigger and bigger drops.

As height and speed of your drops increases, it will help to land with your feet closer together and to be more adaptable with your arms.

Note: Dropping into a roll is not the same as a dive roll. When you're dropping from a height, your feet will still make contact first.

Side Roll

The side roll is good for preventing injury when falling in a weird direction.

The technique is very similar to that of a forward roll, except that you will roll on a more horizontal angle across your back. The exact rolling path will also depend on the angle you are falling at.

As you fall, use your hands to help control your movement. Ensure that you clear your arm/shoulder and land somewhere on your back.

Use the momentum to create as smooth a roll as possible, and then come back onto your feet.

Back Roll

When you're first learning the back roll, it helps to do the forward roll first. Do the forward roll and stop before getting to your feet, then roll back using the same line as you rolled forward on.

Roll forward and back a few times to get the feeling.

When you're ready, you can back roll and come up to stand. At the end of your back roll, continue to go over your shoulder.

Use your hands to push yourself up a little so you can get onto your feet.

When you're back rolling from a drop, always try to get absorb the landing with your legs as much as possible. Landing with one foot in behind the other will make going into the roll much easier.

Lower yourself down as much as possible and then go into the roll.

Get back to your feet as previously described.

It is important to practice rolling until it's an instinctive reaction, and then to continue to practice it regularly with all variations (jumping, momentum, both sides of the body, landing at different angles, etc.).

BREAK-FALLING

Break-falling is primarily a martial arts technique used to lessen the impact when you fall. It's not very conducive to parkour because it disrupts "flow"—once you break-fall, you stop—but it's necessary to learn for safety reasons.

Break-falling works by spreading the impact of the fall across a larger portion of your body. It may still hurt a little, but much less damage will be done.

Rolling is always preferable to break-falling, since it's also a quick way to get back on your feet. However, there will be times when the safety roll is not feasible, such as when there's a lack of space. This is when the break-fall comes in very handy.

There are a few different ways to break-fall. In the Survival Fitness Plan, the judo method is used, because judo is a martial art that makes heavy use of throwing people to the ground. Therefore, they really need to know how to break-fall well.

Note: After any break-fall, you can return to your feet with the safety roll, or just use your hands to help you stand.

Practice break-falling on soft ground, such as grass, gym mats, sand, etc. It will also help to breathe out as you hit the ground.

In all break-falls, there are two big things to watch out for.

1. Do not stick your hand down. For many people, this is a natural reaction when falling, but doing it will focus the impact of the fall onto a single point, which is likely to cause injury.
2. Protect your head from hitting the ground. This is done differently depending on the break-fall, but the basic idea is to move your head or face away from the ground.

Back Break-Fall

Stand with your feet about shoulder-width apart.

Squat down as low as you can and tuck your chin to your chest. Tucking your chin will keep you from hitting the back of your head on the ground.

Fall onto your back and arms, allowing a slight roll, but don't roll back too much.

If you stop the roll "dead," it will put too much pressure on your body, but you don't want your legs to go too far towards your head for the same reason.

Having your feet turned out a little and your knees slightly bent will help you to control this.

Your arms will splay out at about 45°.

Side Break-Fall

From a standing position, step forward with your right leg and do a single-leg squat as you bring your left leg through. The more you bend the leg, the closer you'll be to the ground before landing.

Get as low to the ground as you can, tuck your chin to your chest, and then fall onto the left side of your torso/back and on the whole of your left arm at about a 45° angle from your body, palm facing down. Your legs will probably go in the air.

Allow your legs to come back to the ground, finishing in a comfortable position, but not splayed too wide or crossed.

Forward Break-Fall

With the front break-fall, you fall directly forward and land on your forearms.

Start on your knees so you're low to the ground. Put your arms in front of your face in an upside-down V.

As you fall towards the ground, tense your core and take the impact on your forearms. Try not to let your belly hit the ground and turn your face to the side.

Once you are confident, do this from a standing position. Spread your legs so you can be lower to the ground.

Eventually, you'll be able to do it from a full standing position and with a little jump.

Forward Roll Break-Fall

The forward roll break-fall is useful to know when you go to roll but there is an obstacle ahead preventing you from standing up.

Do a forward safety roll as normal, but instead of coming onto your feet, stop in the side break-fall position.

From there, you can do a backwards safety roll to get back to your feet.

With all break-falls, once you're confident in your technique, you can try doing them with less and less of a squat. You can also try them in different scenarios, such as falling off a chair.

WARM-UPS AND CONDITIONING

Use warm-up exercises to prepare your body for vigorous activity. A proper warm-up is essential to prevent injury.

Conditioning will strengthen your muscles and improve endurance.

Most of the exercises in this section are both warm-up and conditioning rolled into one.

They are all also useful as parkour movements in their own right, as well as being "stepping stones" to the more advanced parkour techniques outlined in this manual.

CATWALK

The catwalk is a form of quadrupedal movement. Quadrupedal movement is the act of moving on all fours. Other types of quadrupedal movement described in this book include side sapiens and ground kongs.

All types of quadrupedal movement have their practical uses, and they also make great warm-up/conditioning exercises.

The catwalk is useful when you have to traverse ledges, rails, etc., or to get through or under small areas. It gives you more balance and control on the obstacle, and it lowers your profile, which makes it great to use for escape and evasion.

Start by getting down on your hands (flat palms) and feet, with your left hand in front of your right hand, and your right foot in front of your left foot. Your hands and feet should form a line. As you move forward you want to maintain this line as much as possible. When you're first starting, it will help to follow an actual line on the ground. When you're on a ledge or rail, you will have little choice anyway.

To move forward, first move your rear hand to the front, then your rear foot to the front. Repeat this. Start slowly, with small steps, and ensure that you transfer the weight evenly between your arm and legs —front and back, left and right.

For stability, keep three points of contact with the surface at all times.

Once your movement is coordinated, concentrate on perfecting your posture. Make yourself as level as possible, from your hips to your head. Keep your back flat and your head forward.

Don't stretch yourself out, bring your knees too close to your body, or stick your bum out.

When you need a rest, crouch. Do not put your knees on the ground.

Progress further and work different muscles by cat-walking backwards, up and down stairs, getting really low, on ledges, on rails, etc.

BALANCE

Balance is very important in parkour. One way to improve it is with rail work, or doing various exercises on a rail. There are a couple described in this chapter, but you can create your own also. Rail work also has other advantages, such as:

- Building resilient joints to help sustain the stresses of high-impact jumping and landing.
- Cultivating body awareness.
- Improving all-over body strength.
- Increasing your focus levels.

Ideally, you'll want to be able to do all these exercises on a round rail since it is (in most places) the hardest, most common urban structure to balance on. Progress to this by starting on the ground, then moving to ledges, flat planks, square rails, etc.

Squatting

First, you need to be able to get into the squat position on the ground.

If you do not have the flexibility for this, then there are a couple of stretches you can do.

These two stretches are excerpted from the book *Curing Yoga* by Aventuras DeViaje.

www.SurvivalFitnessPlan.com/Curing-Yoga

Seated Forward Bend

Avoid this if you have an ankle, arm, hip, and/or shoulder injury.

Start in a seated position with your legs extended straight out in front of you. Inhale and raise your arms up to the sky, with your palms facing each other. Lengthen your torso through your fingers and the crown of your head.

As you exhale, bend at the hips, lowering your upper body to your legs. Grab your ankles, feet, or toes.

Push out through your heels as you pull your toes back towards you.

You can use your arms to pull yourself closer to your legs. If you have more flexibility, reach your hands in front of your feet. If you're having difficulties, bend your knees enough so that you can reach your feet and place your head on your knees.

When you're ready, slowly roll up your spine back into the seated position.

Downward Dog

Place your hands and knees on the floor, with your palms directly underneath your shoulders and fingers facing forward. Your knees are shoulder-width apart and your feet are directly behind them. Have your back flat.

As you inhale, tuck in your toes so you are on the balls of your feet. Keep your palms shoulder width apart and spread your fingers apart, with your middle fingers facing forward.

Press into your hands and lift your hips towards the sky.

Push your hips up and back. Your chest should move towards your thighs. Keep your arms straight, but don't lock your elbows.

Keep your spine straight as you lift up through your tailbone.

Stretch the backs of your legs by pressing your heels to the floor. Keep your back flat. Your legs should be straight (knees not locked) or with a small bend at the knees.

Let your head dangle freely.

Rail Squat

Once you can do at least ten squats on the ground, try them on the rail. You can hold onto it to start with. When you've found your balance/confidence, let go. It may help to focus your gaze on a single point in front of you.

Stand slowly. Keep standing on the rail for a few seconds. Once you're ready, go down and up again.

Rail Walk

The next step is to walk. Walk forward a bit, then turn around and walk back.

It will help to start on something easier than a rail. At the most basic level, you can just follow a line on the ground, then use a wide plank and thinner ones as you progress.

The key to keeping balance is correct posture. As you walk, keep your chest up, knees slightly bent, and your bum over your heels. Take each step toes first.

Go slowly to begin with, use "airplane arms" until you're confident, and stop to regain balance when needed.

Try walking backwards as well.

Note: In a real-life scenario, you would most likely use a monkey traverse or catwalk on the rail, as these two methods would give you more control and a lower profile.

Rail Balance Routine

Once you can do all the things above, you can put them into a short rail-balancing routine that you can do regularly. Jump up on to the rail, get balanced in the squat position, do a few squats on the rail, stand, walk forward, turn around, walk backwards, and catwalk. Increase difficulty with inclined rails.

Slacklining

When you want to become a beast of balance, you can move from the rail to slacklining. Just do the rail balancing routine on the slackline.

Slacklining is basically tightrope walking but most people will use a dynamic (stretchy), flat, broad (a few inches) piece of webbing tied between two anchor points, usually trees.

To learn more about slackening, including the various types and how to set a line up, visit:

Slackline.hivefly.com/slacklining-for-beginners-step-by-step

SIDE SAPIENS

Side sapiens (a.k.a. side monkeys) are a type of quadrupedal movement that are used as a progression to the reverse vault.

They are also useful in their own right as a way to displace momentum (such as when you're landing from a drop) and/or to continue flow into your next movement.

Start in a low squat position.

Reach your arms out across your body to your left and plant them firmly on the ground. Your right hand should land first, followed closely by your left.

Keep your arms strong and use them to support your body weight as you bring your legs to your left. Your right foot should land first, followed closely by your left, so that you end up back in the low squat position.

Engage your core and land with control. Land lightly with your feet and as quietly as you can.

Repeat this movement a few times and then go back the other way.

This is also good to practice on ledges and rails.

For more of a challenge, you can do this exercise with straight legs.

GROUND KONGS

Ground kongs are a type of quadrupedal movement used as a progression to the kong vault.

They are also useful in their own right as a way for you to displace momentum (such as when you're landing from a drop) and/or to continue flow into your next movement.

Start in a low squat position.

Reach forward and plant both your hands firmly on the ground.

Keep your arms strong and use them to support your body weight as you bring your legs up to your hands (or as close as you can).

Engage your core and land with control. Land lightly with your feet and as quietly as you can.

Repeat this movement a few times.

When you are confident, practice on ledges and rails. As you build strength you can try to cover more ground.

You can also do ground kongs backwards which will target a different set of muscles.

PULL-UPS

Pull-ups are an excellent all-body exercise. Doing them regularly will help condition you for wall climb-ups and, eventually, muscle-ups.

Grab the bar with a grip slightly wider than shoulder-width apart and with your palms facing away from you.

Let yourself hang all the way down.

Pull yourself up by pulling your shoulder blades down and together. Keep your chest up and pull up until your chin is above the bar. Touch your chest to it.

As you are pulling up, keep your body in a vertical line. Do not swing. Concentrate on isolating your back and biceps.

Pause at the top, and then lower yourself back down into the hanging position.

RUNNING AND JUMPING

This section contains techniques to do with running and jumping over or between obstacles without coming into contact with them. It also includes explanations of parkour runs and games.

SPRINTING

In parkour, you sprint in between overcoming obstacles.

Sprinting is an efficient form of exercise. It's far more effective to do multiple short sprints than it is to run/jog long distance. Sprinting gives the same health benefits in a much shorter time, as well as other benefits that jogging or running do not offer.

Unlike jogging or running, sprinting creates explosive power, which is very important in parkour. Sprinting is very functional and much more useful than long-distance jogging when it comes to escaping from danger.

If for some reason you do need to run for a long distance, practicing parkour in general you will give you the endurance you need to do so —more than you would have if you just went jogging every day.

Proper Running Technique

Using proper running technique will enable you to go faster and longer while expending less energy.

When running (sprinting), keep your elbows bent at 90° and move your hand from your pocket to your chin.

Move your knees and elbows in unison. As you drive your elbows back, bring your knees up. Then, as your hand goes to your chin, drive your leg back down.

Be sure to bring your hand from your pocket to your chin. The further back your elbows go, the higher your knees will go.

Keep your chin level, eyes focused forward, core engaged, shoulders relaxed, and torso upright (opposed to leaning forward).

This posture keeps your mass vertical, which means your feet will strike the ground with more force and you will produce more speed.

Even when you get tired, always keep correct running form.

Mouth Breathing

You use up a lot of oxygen while running, which you need to replace efficiently.

Breathing through your mouth allows more oxygen to enter your body. It also prevents you from clenching your teeth together, which may cause headaches.

Note: When you're breathing normally, or if you have to run in high pollution, it is better to breathe through your nose. Your nose is your body's air treatment system. It filters, humidifies, and warms the air before it reaches the rest of your body.

Belly Breathing

Learn this first by lying on your back. As you exhale, use your stomach muscles to help expel all the air from your lungs. To inhale, just relax your stomach muscles and let the air come in.

Once you're comfortable with belly breathing, use it while sprinting.

Breathing in Step

Breathing in time to your steps is the easiest way to regulate the rhythm of your breath. This is useful for monitoring and controlling certain things while you are running.

At a normal run rate (not sprinting), stay at a 2:2 ratio. That is, inhale over two steps and then exhale over two steps. During harder runs, you may need to change the ratio to 1:2 or 2:1.

When you go up a hill, maintain the same breath ratio as you were using before the hill. This ensures you'll use the same amount of energy to get over the hill.

To fix a side-stitch while running, slow your breathing to a deeper 3:3 rhythm.

Another way to fix a stitch is to expand and contract your diaphragm in the opposite direction from usual. When you breathe in, make your stomach contract, and when you exhale make your stomach expand.

Note: Breathing at a 1:1 ratio or faster may lead to hyperventilation, and breathing at a 3:3 ratio or slower means you may not get enough oxygen into your body.

EVASIVE RUNNING

Evasive running is the ability to maneuver out of the way of an oncoming or stationary obstacle while running.

When learning evasive running, use a running speed slightly slower than sprinting. You want to be quick, but not so quick that you will get injured while performing the movement.

Train to evade humans, as they will be the hardest to outsmarting. You want to go in whichever direction is hardest for your opponent to go.

As you approach your opponent, look him in the eye. This will make it harder for him to predict where you are going, and he will probably think you're charging straight at him.

If your opponent is square on with you but is flat-footed (left picture), it should be fairly easy to pass him on either side.

If he has one side forward more (right image), evade him by going to the other side of his body. It will probably be his weaker side, and it will be harder for him to maneuver in that direction. In the scenario in the picture on the right, you would maneuver to the woman's left. since her right foot is forward.

If an opponent angles away from you, then go the opposite way. In the picture, the woman has stepped to her left with her right foot. You would evade her by moving to her right, to the outside of her.

You can practice this with a friend. Have your friend face you square on as you run towards him. When you are close, your friend should step toward you and you should evade in the best direction.

You could also practice against a stationary object. Run towards it and evade it on either side at the last moment.

HURDLES

Hurdles are often neglected in parkour, but they are the fastest way to pass an obstacle, and sometimes—if you're dealing with chain-link fences or hedges, for example—the only way. You should use them whenever possible. They are best used over small obstacles that you are confident you can clear.

The mechanics of hurdles can be learned with a couple of drills.

Trail Leg Drill

The trail leg drill teaches you to lift your rear leg up and to the outside as opposed to coming straight through.

Face a wall just over one natural step away, and lean your palms flat against it. Bring your left leg straight up behind you and then bring your knee to the front, parallel to your hip.

Keep your heel directly behind your knee far as you can, and then snap your foot back down to the ground.

Do this drill ten times on each side of your body.

Front-Leg Drill

The front-leg drill teaches you to lean forward which is very important for momentum.

Stand facing a wall, just over one natural step away from it.

Thrust your front leg straight up and into the wall. Really lean into it. As you bring your leg up, reach forward with your opposite hand.

Do this drill ten times on each side of your body.

The Hurdle

After you have practiced those two drills, you can try an actual hurdle.

Approach an obstacle with enough speed that you're confident you'll clear it.

Thrust your lead foot and opposite arm forward as you kick your rear leg back.

As your body comes over the obstacle, bring your rear knee to the front, parallel to your hip.

Land on your lead foot and continue running forward.

PRECISION JUMPING

Precision jumping is a fundamental parkour skill in which you jump from one stationary point to another. It is important to learn how to be precise with your landings so that you can land safely on smaller obstacles such as ledges, handrails, and walls.

When you're doing precision jumping, your aim is to land exactly on your intended landing spot, with no extra momentum in either direction—that is, without stumbling forward.

Begin with your feet together and bend your knees a little, so you're in a semi-crouched position.

Move your arms behind you as you shift your weight to the balls of your feet.

Lean forward. The greater the distance you need to jump, the more you need to lean.

As you jump, throw your arms forwards and upwards. Your energy will travel up your legs, through your torso, and into your hands.

Aim to arc up and then come down on to the landing area, landing on the balls of your feet as quietly as you can. Land on both feet at the same time, just as you would in the safety tap.

As you build confidence, start jumping from farther back and with small level differences, such as onto a curb.

You can also try high to low, to/from rails, etc.

Note: When jumping onto smaller platforms (such as handrails) it is extra important that you aim to land on the balls of your feet. This way, if you slip a little then you have the whole of your foot to recover. If you land on your heels and slip, you will probably fall.

Jumping Larger Gaps

Note: It's a good idea to learn the crane landing before attempting larger gaps just in case you jump short.

Practice precision jumping over larger gaps on the ground first to see if you can make it. This is also useful to improve your distance.

Use lines on the road or any other type of marker, so you can take off and land on exact points.

When doing longer precision jumps, focus more on extending your body. Once you are in the air, bring your knees forward.

Push your feet towards the landing point and land as softly as you can.

Running Precision Jumps

When precision jumping over very large gaps, you can use the running precision jump. The running precision jump is exactly what it sounds like—a precision jump with a run up, as opposed to leaping from a stationary position.

The running precision jump uses a one-foot take off, but you still land with both feet, in the same way as in a standing precision jump.

Since you are jumping with much more momentum, sticking the landing becomes more difficult. Many people find they jump too far and/or stumble forward when landing.

CRANE LANDING

The crane landing is used when you want to land on obstacles that are just a bit too far (either in height or distance) to precision jump onto, but are still small enough that you don't feel the need to cat-hang or vault.

Your intention should be to have one of your feet land on top of the obstacle while the other one supports you down the front of it.

Prepare to jump just like you would in a precision jump.

The decision about making a precision jump may be made either before you jump or mid-air.

Put the foot that you intend to land on top of the obstacle with in front.

Your front foot should land on top while your rear foot should push against the front of the obstacle to prevent you from falling back.

Once you're stable, bring your rear foot up onto the obstacle.

STRIDING

Parkour striding, a.k.a. bounding, is leaping from one foot to another in succession. It is useful for running across elevated obstacles.

Approach the stride like a running precision jump. Run up and take off from one foot. Stretch your legs out front and back.

As your lead leg lands, you want your center of gravity to be over your foot so you can push off into the next stride. If you're too far forward or back, it will mess up your momentum.

It will help to get your arms and leg in sync, just as you would if you were walking.

You can use this arm swing to generate more power. The further the distance between your obstacles, the more you should swing your arms.

STRIDE TO SAFETY STEP

The stride to safety step is used to stride over a gap onto a ledge (or something similar) and then safely move down a level, such as to the ground. It's actually a combination of two other parkour techniques, striding and the safety step-through (a.k.a. down step).

Note: Before you attempt the stride to safety step, you should know how to stride and how to do the safety vault (the safety step-through is covered as part of the safety vault).

Run up to the first ledge and stride off it as usual.

Land on the second ledge one foot first. Most people find it easiest to land on the opposite foot from they took off with, but either foot is possible.

As you land, lean out a little to the opposite side of the foot you landed on. This is so you have enough room for your other leg to come through.

Allow your leg to absorb most of the impact, and then place your hand on the ledge, fingers pointing out to your side.

Your other leg should come through between your hand and foot so you can push yourself away from the edge.

Here is a view from the front.

This demonstrates leaving off one leg and then landing on the opposite one, which is the way most people prefer to do it.

You could also leave off one leg and then land on the same one. Experiment to see which you prefer.

It also shows a person going from lower to higher, but you can do it between surfaces of the same level, or from higher to lower.

DIVE ROLL

The dive roll is used to prevent injury when you're coming down on your head.

In most cases, this is intentional in the way of diving over an obstacle, but may also be used in accidental falls where you are low to the ground and don't have the room to land feet-first—if your foot clips on the obstacle while you're hurdling, for example.

Note: In the case that you fell (or were thrown) off something high, landing feet-first and doing a safety roll, if possible, is your best option.

Ensure you are proficient at the safety roll before attempting the dive roll.

Avoid doing the dive roll on hard ground, even when you're proficient.

The technique for doing the dive roll is very similar to the one for the forward roll, but there is a lot more impact and momentum. In addition, you are coming toward your head as opposed to landing on your feet first.

Start by practicing the forward roll from a handstand. You don't need to be great at handstands, you just have to get to the right angle for a moment so you can go into the roll.

Lower yourself with your arms, then lean forward slightly to tuck your head as you go into the roll.

Keep your body strong (arms, core, legs, and neck) as you allow your body to "collapse" into the roll.

Once you're comfortable, you can start jumping into the dive roll from a standing position.

Kick your leg back as you jump to help get your hips over.

As you hit the ground, absorb some of the impact with your arms by keeping them strong while allowing them to collapse. Use your arms to ensure you get over your head.

Use the momentum to flow onto your back and into the roll.

Next try it with a short run up, and then try jumping off with two feet.

Slowly progress until you are doing a full dive roll.

Dive and stretch out like a cat.

Absorb the impact with your arms.

Tuck your head as you go into the roll.

Train at this level until the movement is instinctive, then progress by jumping higher and over things.

When jumping over things, ensure your hips clear the obstacle and your legs/feet follow on the same path.

PARKOUR RUNS

A parkour run is when you put your parkour skills into practical use. Basically, the idea is to go from one point to another in the most efficient manner. All you need is a few basic techniques and you can start.

To begin with you may just want to do a short run with two or three techniques put together in a flow. You can suss out a site first so you know exactly what you want to do.

Try different things to see what works best (fastest and most efficiently) for you. Practice each technique individually, and then put them together. Gradually get faster and faster. Eventually you want to be able to go from point A to point B long distance without having to suss it out first.

Good runs are those in which the transition between techniques is smooth. Once you're confident, your aim should be to move as quickly and quietly as possible, adapting to your environment as you go.

PARKOUR GAMES

Parkour games are a good way to vary your training. They are great for kids and adults alike, and most of them are just adaptations of games you probably already know. Here are a couple of examples.

Horse

One person does a technique or short run and the others have to replicate it. If they are unable to replicate it, they get a letter "H."

Once they have used up all their letters (HORSE), they are out of the game. Take turns being the person who performs the technique that the others have to replicate.

Of course, the word you spell can be anything, such as PARKOUR.

Quadrupedal Tag

Play a game of tag in which you're only allowed to use different types of quadrupedal movement (ground kongs, side sapiens, cat-walking, etc.).

This concept can easily be applied to many other games, such as capture the flag. You can also just play normal tag, but use your parkour skills.

Lava Pit

A childhood favorite where you pretend the ground is molten lava. Move around, being sure not to fall in. This is easily combined with tag.

VAULTS

Technically a vault is any type of movement that involves overcoming an obstacle, but in this section it only refers to those movements in which you make contact with the obstacle you are going over.

SAFETY VAULT

The safety vault is used to pass a relatively low and short obstacle in front of you, such as a waist-height wall.

The safety vault is the very first vault learned in Survival Fitness Plan Parkour Training. This is because it is the easiest to learn and the safest to do.

It is also a necessary technique to know so you can progress to the similar but faster speed vault, the reverse safety vault, and the stride-to-safety-step techniques.

An easy way to learn the safety vault is by numbering your hands and feet. It will help you to remember the order of placement.

1. Left hand.
2. Right leg.
3. Left leg.
4. Right hand.

Take it slow to begin with. Get the pattern into your head, and eventually into your muscle memory.

Approach the obstacle and place your left hand (#1) on it. Next, place your right leg (#2). Stretch it out far enough to allow your left leg (#3) to pass between your left hand and right leg.

Step straight through with your left leg. Keep your right arm (#4) up so you can pass your leg through easier.

Here is what it looks like from the front.

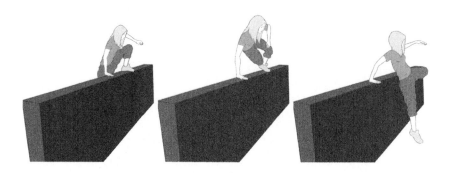

Practice on both sides of your body.

When you add speed, your #1 leg doesn't have to push off that much. It becomes just a touch on top of the obstacle so you can gauge where it is.

As you run up to the obstacle, be sure not to stop in preparation for the vault. Stride directly onto it, and go up and over the object in an arc.

Land with your chest above or in front of your foot, and use your #1 and #2 to push the object behind you so you get more forward momentum. At the same time, reach down to the floor with your #3 leg.

SPEED VAULT

The speed vault is used to quickly pass over small to medium-sized obstacles that are too big for you to hurdle over. Before attempting the speed vault, you should be proficient at the safety vault.

Note: If you're approaching an obstacle at an angle, use the lazy vault.

The speed vault is basically the same as a safety vault, except you don't let your foot touch the wall. You can do the following exercise to get your legs coordinated for this.

If you want to place your left hand on the obstacle, raise your right leg straight out to your right. Quickly follow it with your left. Tap your right foot with your left in the air.

Be sure to raise your right and then your left, as opposed to jumping with both legs at the same time. Your left foot should land back on the ground first.

This leg kicking motion is what you use to pass the obstacle, except without tapping your feet.

Approach the object with some speed, so you can clear it. As with most vaults, you want to arc over the obstacle. Run and kick your legs up. Once you're in the air, place your hand on the obstacle (fingers facing forwards) and push up and back to help get your chest and legs through.

Keep your chest pointing forward, and don't hold onto the wall too long; otherwise, it will focus your momentum in a different direction (as opposed to straight ahead).

Switch your legs through while you are in the air and land on your inside foot first—that is, the foot on same side as the hand you have on the wall. Your chest should be facing forward and in front of your leading leg as you land. Be sure to push the obstacle behind you before landing.

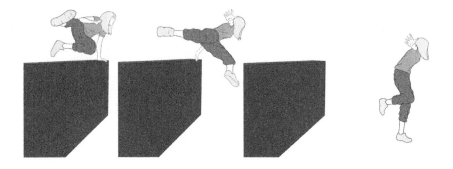

Note: If you want to exit in a direction other than straight ahead, try to face your chest in the direction you want to go and use your hand on the wall as a pivot point.

TURN VAULT

The turn vault can be used to pass over a rail, wall, fence, ledge, etc. in a swift and safe manner. Besides passing over as usual, another common use of the turn vault is to cat-hang (or just hang) over the other side of an obstacle before dropping down.

It's a good idea to learn the safety vault before attempting the turn vault. This will give you a basic understanding of the body mechanics needed to get over an obstacle and help to build your confidence.

When first learning the turn vault, do it over a rail rather than a wall. If you're worried about clearing the height, you can first try it at the end of the rail so your legs can just come around the end if needed.

Start with a rail about waist height.

Place your hands on the rail a comfortable distance apart (shoulder-width is usually good), with one hand facing up and the other facing down. Your legs will go in the direction of the hand facing down, which is the hand you will take off the rail.

Squat back so your arms are almost straight, and then push up with your legs while pulling with your arms to arc up and over the rail. Your legs should swing around to the side.

Your chest should come over the bar first. As your legs come over the bar, release your hand so you can complete the 180° spin.

Once you're on the other side place, your hand back on the bar in an overhand position, at about the same distance as it was originally. As you're doing this, you also want to be looking at where to place your feet.

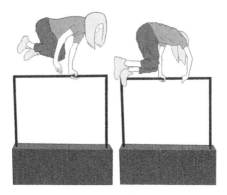

As you come down to land, lean back a little and place your feet on the target. Leaning back allows the energy to get pushed through your feet, which will give you a good grip.

Don't worry if you can't get your hand and foot in the right place on the other side right away. Just keep practicing.

Once you can do the turn vault on a rail smoothly, you can progress to using a wall/ledge. You'll need to adjust your hand positioning since you can't grab under a wall. Somewhere close to 90° to the side is good.

Come over in the usual way, but use less speed, so you can hold yourself up on the other side.

Once you're stable, you can drop down into a cat-hang or do whatever else you want.

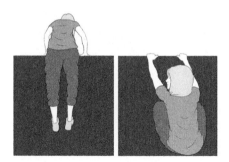

Once you're confident/have built enough strength, you can use more speed and go straight into a cat-hang.

REVERSE SAFETY VAULT

The reverse safety vault (a.k.a. reverse step vault) is a good progression technique to use to work up to the reverse vault, but it also has a lot of practical uses in its own right.

If you're backed up against an obstacle, you can use the reverse safety vault to pass over it without having to turn to face it. Then you can either land to face your aggressor or land facing away so you can run. You can also use it to back out of numerous types of forward-facing vaults if you see danger on the other side.

Stand with your back to the obstacle and place your right hand on it, fingers facing forward. Hop up onto it, with your left foot making contact.

Push off with your left foot so that you turn to your left and land on the other side, facing away from the obstacle. Land on your right foot first.

Eventually you want to be able to do this smoothly, without having to look at your foot as you come up onto the obstacle.

Practice it so you stay facing the same way as well. Instead of pushing off with your left foot to spin, just place your right foot onto the ground.

LAZY VAULT

The lazy vault is useful when approaching a small to medium-sized obstacle at an angle other than straight on, and no matter what speed your approach is.

It can be used when coming in and out on a similar angle, and it can also be adapted to exit on a different angle.

Assuming you are approaching the obstacle from your left, your limbs should go over the wall in this order:

1. Left hand.
2. Left leg.
3. Right leg.
4. Right hand.

This first progression step will help you to get the mechanics of the technique.

Approach the wall on a diagonal and place your left hand (#1) on it as you jump up. Your left leg (#2) should come through, so that you land on the wall with your right foot (#3).

Drop down to the ground, landing on your left foot first (#2), and then continue to run.

Here it is approaching from the opposite side. Your right hand is #1.

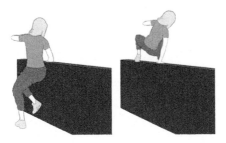

Once you're ready, you can learn the actual lazy vault, which means you will not place your #3 foot on the wall.

Kick your legs up over the wall and bring your hips up.

As you go over, your #4 hand should replace your #2 hand on the obstacle.

Use your #4 hand to help push your hips away from the obstacle so you can continue running.

A "proper" lazy vault is one in which you approach on an angle and exit along the same path. Ensure your limbs go over in the right order and that you land/run out on #2.

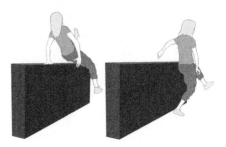

If you want to exit on a different angle, just turn your hips in the direction you want to go while you're still in the air.

If you are exiting on a different angle unintentionally, it may be because you're forgetting to put your #4 hand down.

KONG VAULT

The kong vault (also known as the cat pass, monkey vault, kong leap, etc.) is useful for vaulting longer or higher obstacles. It's a bit more difficult than the previous vaults explained in this book, but is worth the practice because it's extremely useful.

Start on something wide enough to land on but not too high, like a picnic table, and small enough to vault over (eventually).

This first progression exercise is helpful in getting over the fear of hitting your toes on the obstacle.

Stand at one end of the obstacle and place your palms flat on it a little more than shoulder-width apart, with your fingers facing forwards.

Use your arms to support you as you jump up onto the obstacle, landing with your feet between your hands. Move your hands away as needed.

Repeat this exercise until you're comfortable with the mechanics.

When you're ready, try to land further and further forward with your feet by pushing the obstacle back underneath you. The more you push, the further you can go.

Next try starting with some distance between you and the obstacle. Take a one- or two-step run-up, then do the same as before.

Let the momentum help you to get further onto the obstacle.

To get even further, you can run up with a bit more momentum, using one of two take-offs depending on the type of obstacle.

First, try the two-foot punch take off, which most people find easier. It will redirect momentum up, which makes it better for high obstacles.

Start further away from the obstacle than you have been. Run up and hop on one foot.

Land on both feet together, then use the momentum to go into a dive onto the obstacle before completing the vault as normal.

You will need practice to learn where a good distance is for you to land back from the obstacle.

Next, try the split-foot take-off. This take-off has more forward momentum than the two-foot punch take-off, which makes it better for longer obstacles.

Start at about the same distance as you did for the two-foot punch take off. Run up and hop on one foot, then land on the opposite one.

Take another quick step then push up with both feet to go into the dive. Complete the vault as before.

Try to get further and further, until you can clear the obstacle.

To get more distance, increase your approach speed and use the split-foot take-off. Kick out your feet to raise your hips, which will help stretch out your dive.

Spot where you want your hands to land, and then push up and forward as your arms make contact.

Land on two feet to begin with, and then progress into landing in a one-two motion so you can resume running.

Once you are comfortable, try the kong vault on higher and/or longer obstacles using the appropriate take-off—the two-foot punch for higher ones and the split foot for longer ones.

REVERSE VAULT

The reverse vault is useful when you have a lot of momentum but not enough space to dive or swing your leg. This may be because two obstacles are very close together, or because someone has swung you with your back towards an obstacle.

There are two good ways to learn the reverse vault.

The first is to get faster and faster at the reverse safety vault. The more you do it, the less you'll need to put the weight on your foot, until eventually you will be able to get all the way over the obstacle and land on the other side in a standard reverse vault.

The second way is to build up from side sapiens. For detailed instructions on how to do side sapiens, see the section on warm-ups and conditioning.

Once you are comfortable with side sapiens, try the following twisting variation of it. Face forward, and then place your hands as if doing side sapiens, but at a 90° angle.

Use your arms to support your weight as you turn in a circle, until you're facing forward again.

This twisting motion variation of side sapiens can also be adapted to save you if you're sitting on something and fall (or are pushed) backwards.

The next progression is to do side sapiens over an obstacle.

When you are ready, add a full twist as you come down out of the move.

Land on the foot closest to the obstacle first, and keep spinning until you're facing away from it.

Finally, start the twist from the beginning.

Finish by landing in the same way as before.

Practice this vault immediately after other vaults when the obstacles are close together or while you're being flung into one.

An opponent grabs you and begins to fling you into an obstacle.

When you are about a step away from the obstacle, start to turn your back to it.

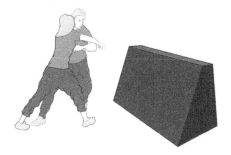

Place your hand on the obstacle first to help gauge distance and direct momentum as you vault over it.

WALL TECHNIQUES

This section covers all the techniques that are predominantly associated with walls. They are mostly to do with overcoming obstacles that are too big to vault.

CAT LEAP TO CAT HANG

The cat leap (a.k.a. the arm jump, arm leap, etc.) to cat hang is a commonly used technique in which you jump towards a vertical obstacle (cat leap) and hang off it (cat hang).

The standard cat leap is from a precision or running jump, but other techniques, such as a kong vault or a lache, are also often used.

Once in the cat hang, you can choose to drop down, climb up, cat to cat, etc. The cat hang is also very useful in its own right, since it can be used to lower yourself to the ground. You can do a turn vault to cat hang and then drop down.

When first learning the cat leap to cat hang, start from a stationary position fairly close to the obstacle.

As you jump toward the obstacle, lean back a little and bring your feet and hands out in front of you. Arc into your landing and connect with the obstacle feet-first so that your feet can absorb the impact.

Keep a little space between your feet as you land, so that if you fall back you have more control.

If it is a low obstacle, avoid landing too high on it otherwise you will find it harder to grab the top.

Note: It is very important to connect with the obstacle feet-first. If you don't, you'll probably just slam into it.

Once you have grabbed onto the top of the obstacle, you can straighten your arms so you are "crouching" against the wall. This is the cat hang. From here, you can drop down or climb up.

If dropping down, kick away from the obstacle a little bit and turn away from it on your way down. Land with a safety tap or roll.

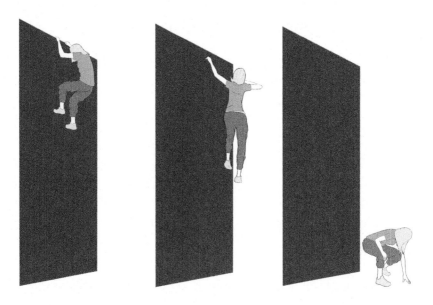

Practice with different heights, distances, etc., so you get used adjusting your jump in different circumstances.

CAT TO CAT

The cat to cat is when you leap from one cat hang to another one on an opposing obstacle.

Before learning the cat to cat, you need to know the cat hang.

Find two obstacles that directly face one another. This makes it easier to learn to begin with.

Go into a cat hang on the first obstacle.

Turn you head to spot where you're going to land, and push off with one of your legs as you let go with your hands.

Immediately turn to face the second obstacle and reach out with your other leg (the opposite of the one you pushed off with) so it's ready to absorb the impact before you take a grip with your hands to land in a cat hang.

Once you're confident, practice with different angles, heights, cat to precision, cat to crane, cat to lache, etc.

In all cases, the main thing is to be aware of is how your feet and hands hit the wall.

When you're going from low to high, you want to get a lot of pressure into the wall, so that your feet don't slip as you push your body up.

When you're going from high to low, make sure that you still get your feet out in front of you and that you're lowering yourself into the landing with your chest back. This will keep you from hitting your face.

TIC-TAC

A tic-tac is when you push your foot off an obstacle on an angle. It's a fairly simple technique that can be used to help you clear gaps, leap over obstacles, gain height, or quickly redirect your momentum.

A horizontal wall run is a progression of the tic-tac in which you take multiple steps along the wall, as opposed to just one.

To begin with, just get used to how the obstacle feels under your foot. Walk up to the obstacle, place your foot on it, and then push off in a slight upward manner so you arc back onto the ground. Land on the foot opposite the one you pushed off with first and then continue to walk away.

You can either focus your tic-tac on pushing away from the obstacle or pushing along it, so experiment with both by facing your chest and shoulders towards your destination.

Next, start to add some momentum and try to get increasing distance and/or height.

The more momentum you have, the harder you can push off the wall and the higher and/or farther you will be able to get. As well, the higher you place your foot on the obstacle, the more lift and distance you will achieve.

Once you're confident, you can start doing it over objects.

Concentrate on your foot placement so you can get enough leverage off the wall to clear the object.

Then try with multiple steps. This is where the tic-tac turns into the horizontal wall run.

Approach at a smaller angle between you and the wall. First try with two steps, then three or more.

The tic-tac can also be used to help you get over higher obstacles.

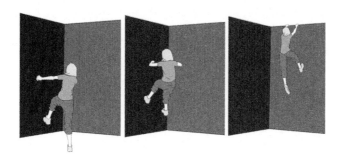

WALL CLIMB-UP

The wall climb-up is used to pull yourself from a hanging position up onto a wall quickly and efficiently.

When you're first learning, it will help to use the momentum from a cat leap or wall run to help get up the wall. Eventually, you'll want to be able to do it from a static hang.

Start on a wall you can easily cat leap to cat hang to, so that you can get the most out of your momentum.

As soon as you have a grip on the obstacle, use your feet to push your hips back as you pull up and in with your arms. Push your feet into the obstacle, not down. Try to straighten your highest leg.

Your leg push and arm pull should be one smooth motion. The aim is to get your chest above the top of the obstacle.

As your chest comes over, you need to transition from having your hands hanging to having them on top. For most people, this is the hardest part of the climb-up.

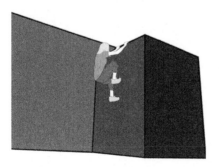 

Using the momentum from the push/pull, quickly take the weight off your hands and pop them on top of the obstacle, so that your palms are on it. The more you can push against the obstacle and the more momentum you have, the easier it will be.

When you're first learning, you can do the transition one arm at a time and then progress to doing them together when you're ready.

Once your hands are on top, push up. Keep your chest forward so you don't fall back. To stand on the obstacle, use one of your feet to kick out a little.

Bring your other foot up on top. Avoid using your elbows and knees to help you.

 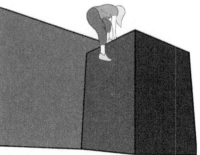

Alternatively, you can do the wall pop-up to stand.

Once you can do the wall climb-up, try doing it from a static hang. Push your body against the obstacle a little to help pop your hips back.

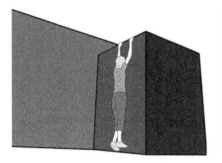 

As your legs swing back in, place one foot on the wall and then get your other leg as high as possible so you can transition into the wall climb-up.

 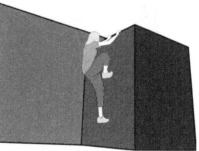

Correct technique is what will get you on top of an obstacle, but having more strength will make it easier, especially when you're doing it from a static hang. Some useful exercises to help build strength are:

- **Dips.** With your hands in front of your chest to mimic the climb-up, as opposed to being out to your sides.
- **Pull ups.** Standard pull-ups. Not to be confused with chin-ups.
- **Reverse climb-ups.** Start from on top of the wall and slowly lower yourself down by reversing the climb-up action.
- **Super-burpees.** The ultimate all-round conditioning exercise.

- **Traversing.** Hang off an obstacle and traverse around it.

Eventually, you can progress to a one-armed wall climb-up from a static hang.

VERTICAL WALL RUN

Use the vertical wall run to get up tall obstacles.

To practice the vertical wall run, you can use any obstacle that is tall enough. You don't have to be able to reach the top to practice, but if you can, it means you can also practice your wall climb (or other techniques) at the same time. Small wall runs may also be used as part of a wall pop-up.

Initially, you will have to get familiar with your steps so you have the right pacing when approaching the obstacle. After a while, this will become intuitive.

Find a spot where you're comfortable with your leg resting on the obstacle at about hip height. It shouldn't be so close you're pushing in or so far away where you're stretching to reach.

Once you've found that space, you can start to get comfortable with setting a foot on the obstacle and jumping off it. Don't worry about gaining height yet.

Use your strong leg against the obstacle first, as that's the one that's going to have the most impact. Eventually, you'll want to practice on both sides.

As your foot hits the obstacle, push into it in an upward motion. The aim is to get your center of gravity to go up. Do not apply too much downward pressure, as it will cause you to slip. Run into the obstacle and bounce up off it.

Once you're comfortable add some speed so you can get more height. Don't go too fast too soon, or you might just slam into the obstacle.

Jump and plant your foot as high as you can, then quickly kick off. If you're too slow to kick off, you will lose power.

If the obstacle is small, you can try grabbing onto the edge. If not, just touch it at as high a point as you can, keeping in mind that the higher you go, the longer the drop back down will be.

After some practice, you'll be able to recognize how to react according to the obstacle, varying your approach speed, when to jump, how high to plant your foot, etc., accordingly.

Throwing your arms up will give you more reach, as will leading with one arm.

Leaving your hand on the obstacle can be useful to give you a little extra push up, as well as to prevent yourself from slamming into it.

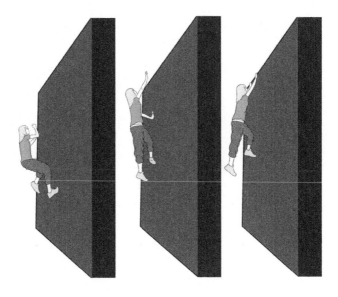

WALL POP-UP

The wall pop-up is used to quickly get over or on top of obstacles that are too high to vault over, but low enough that you don't feel the need to use the wall climb-up.

It can also be used in conjunction with the wall climb. Once you're in the "up" position of the wall climb, use the pop vault to get on top of the wall.

When you're first learning the wall pop-up, do it on an obstacle that's just a little difficult for you to kong vault over.

The first progression for the wall pop-up is to do it with a crane landing.

Do a vertical wall run, but because the obstacle is low, instead of having to hang off it just use your arms give you a little bit of a boost up and then land in a crane landing. A powerful kick off the wall is essential.

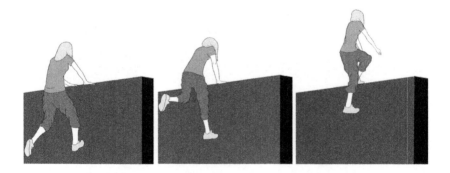

Once you can do that, try bringing both feet up to the side.

Finally, you can do the full wall pop-up by bringing both your feet up to land on top of the obstacle. The movement is like that used in a kong vault.

CORNER WALL RUN

The corner wall run is when you use two walls in a corner to gain extra height. It's like doing a tic-tac off one wall to gain height on the second wall, which you then continue to "run" up.

Before attempting the corner wall run, you should be proficient with the vertical wall run and the tic-tac.

First, get comfortable with doing the tic-tac off one wall and then pushing off the other. You'll need to be quick to react with your feet.

Decide which wall you want to hit first. If it's on your left side, you'll use your left foot to come into it, and if it's on your right side, you'll use your right foot to come into it.

Come in at about a 45° angle and place your foot at about hip level to tic-tac from the first wall into the second.

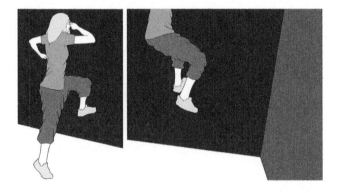

Use your other foot to push back on the second wall (again at about hip level) and then come down to land using a safety tap.

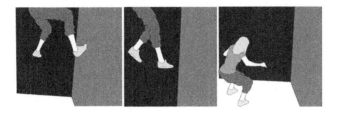

Your arms/hands can help you push on the wall or you can throw them up for more vertical momentum.

Test the angle at which you come in on the first wall so you can get the best push off it.

Continue to practice this gradually, adding more speed so you can get more height. Apply basic wall-run techniques for more vertical lift.

When you're ready, add in the wall run on the second wall so you can reach the top of the obstacle.

Foot placement and explosiveness are the keys. You need lots of power and the right angle into the first tic-tac so you can get more momentum off the second step to continue the wall run.

The above pictures show moving from the left wall to the right and then back to the left to grab the top of the obstacle.

An alternative would be to tic-tac off the right wall then do a standard vertical wall run up the left wall to grab the top.

BAR TECHNIQUES

This section covers techniques that are predominantly associated with bars and that have not been covered in previous sections.

STRAIGHT UNDERBAR

The straight underbar allows you to smoothly pass under and/or between bars or other obstacles, like ledges.

When you're first learning the straight underbar, you want to progress very slowly. If you go too fast too soon, you'll probably end up getting injured.

Find an obstacle with a good-sized gap to pass though. Going from low to high will be easier than going from high to low, as it will give you more control with your feet on the other side.

When doing the underbar, let your feet lead your body and your hands grab the obstacle to help control your body as you go through.

Stand next to the bar and stick one leg through, then the other.

Slowly work your body through. Use this slow speed to become familiar with the distance between your body parts and the obstacle as you go through.

Give extra attention to your back and head, as they are most likely to hit. Be very careful you don't hit your head.

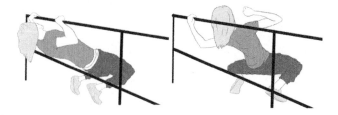

Once you're comfortable, gradually get faster. Try to get straighter as well, rather than coming in side on.

Lead with your feet, lean back a little, and reach forward to grab the bar with your hands so you can pull yourself through.

Lie back as you pull, so your upper torso and head can pass through. Direct your legs upwards.

You can swing your legs slightly to the side if needed to avoid hitting your knees or shins.

Next, try different variations. Practice high to low, low to high, smaller gaps, more speed, coming from the side, gap jump to underbar, etc.

When you're doing gap jumps to underbars, aim with your feet, similar to the way you would with a precision jump. Aim them through the gap, so the rest of your body will follow along the same path.

Don't lean back too much, and as soon as you grab the bar, control the way the rest of your body comes through.

Note: When you're going under (not between) something about chest to head height, doing the underbar is usually unnecessary, but you should still use your hand on the obstacle above you as a guide so that you don't hit your head.

LACHE

The lache is used to swing off a bar (or branch, or anything else you can swing from) and then land in precision, crane, or cat position, or grab onto another bar (lache to lache).

Knowing how to lache properly will allow you to propel yourself a much greater distance from the bar.

The Swing

The most important part of every lache is swinging. Don't just try to swing with your legs. You need to use your shoulders, chest, torso, etc.

Start in a stationary hang on the bar. Get your feet behind you and curve your spine backwards.

Bend your knees to your chest and then push your feet out and up. Keep your arms straight. This is a flowing movement done in an explosive manner.

Lache to Precision

Once you have the correct swing technique, you can attempt the lache to precision. If you don't know how to precision jump yet, learn that first.

As with any precision jump, you need to know where you want to land. Choose any spot (line, crack, etc.) on the ground that you're confident you can reach.

You also need to be able to see that landing spot as you release your hands. To do this, you need to release your hands one at a time.

As your body goes forward, release one of your hands and keep it in front of your eyes. When you gain enough speed, release your second hand and keep your eyes on the line that you're going to land on.

This arm-releasing technique stays the same no matter how far you want to go or what type of lache you're doing. Always release one hand first, then the other.

To precision further, you just need to get more momentum in the swing.

Lache to Lache

For the lache to lache, instead of focusing on a landing point you need to focus on the next bar you'll grab onto.

To do continuous lache to lache, you need to grab the next bar with your legs behind you, so that you maintain enough speed for the next swing.

Start to swing and release your first hand as your legs go in front of you. As you release your second hand, swing your legs behind you. Then catch the bar.

Swing your legs forward again and then repeat the movement, lache to lache to lache.

Lache to Cat Leap

The lache to cat leap is a combination of the lache to precision and the lache to lache. It's lache to precision because you have to land on the wall with your legs, and it's lache to lache because you'll have to grab something with your arms.

If you don't know how to cat leap to cat hang yet, learn that first.

The arm release is the same. Let go with one hand first, then the other. Keep your legs in front of you the whole time, so you can absorb the impact as you land in cat.

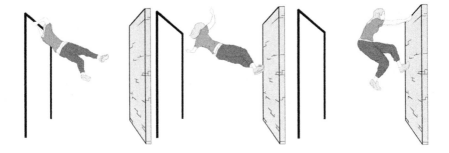

MONKEY TRAVERSE

The monkey traverse (a.k.a. the sloth shimmy) is used to get across long-distance obstacles that you can hang off. It is safer than cat-walking on the bar, and works on rope too.

Hang below the obstacle, suspended by your hands and with both feet crossed over the rope. Your left hand should be in front of your right hand and your right foot should be in front of your left foot.

Keep a slight bend in your arms and engage your core for the whole time you're are traversing.

Start to move your right hand in front of your left hand.

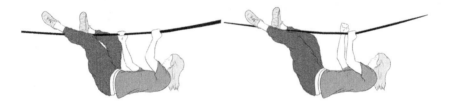

As you take a grip with your right hand, move your left foot in front of your right. Do not slide your feet. Lift them. This will prevent friction burns.

Ensure your feet land ahead of each other and not on top; otherwise, you'll get tangled up.

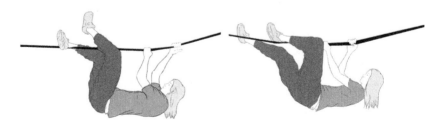

Continue this motion.

MUSCLE-UPS

Muscle-ups are used to get on top of higher obstacles, like over-hanging ledges, in cases where a wall climb-up cannot be used.

You'll need to be proficient at the wall climb-up before attempting the muscle-up, for both technique and conditioning reasons.

The muscle-up is quite a physically demanding exercise. Progressing gradually is the key to success.

Start with the hanging knee to elbow leg raise.

Hang off the bar and pull yourself up slightly to retract your shoulder blades. This will help keep you stable while you're doing the exercise.

Keep your core tight and swing forward a little bit. As your body starts to swing back thrust your knees to your chest.

Next, you need to learn how to use the momentum from the hanging knee to elbow raise to pull yourself over the bar.

Start the hanging knee to elbow leg raise as normal. At the height of your back swing, pull yourself forward and thrust your knees to your chest, while allowing your wrists to rotate over the bar. The wrist movement is very important.

It will help if you have access to a lower bar to practice the movement. If not, then just keep it in mind when doing the muscle-up.

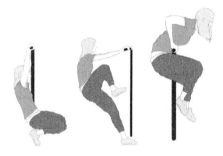

Now you can put everything together to do the muscle-up. It's important to use everything you've learned so far. Remember to keep your core tight.

In addition to retracting your shoulder blades, pull your arms forward a little bit when pulling yourself over the bar.

You can use some chalk to get extra grip, although you probably won't have this luxury in real-life scenarios.

Get some momentum, and then thrust your knees to your chest.

As you do so, ensure your wrists are loosened. At the right moment, pull yourself up over the bar. Push yourself up until your arms are fully extended.

If this was an obstacle, you would bring your foot up and stand, just like in the wall-climb.

If you want to do multiple muscle-ups, you can use the momentum you gain when lowering yourself down to go into the next repetition.

Once you've built more strength, try to do the muscle-up with less and less swing, until you can do it from a dead hang.

You'll also need to practice doing muscle-ups over hanging ledges, where there are no walls for your feet to push against. To do this, you need to adjust your technique a little, since you don't have a bar for your wrist to rotate over. Use the "pop" hand movement you use when doing a wall climb-up.

Dear Reader,

Thank you for reading *Essential Parkour Training*.

If you enjoyed it, please leave a review on Amazon. It helps more than most people think. You can do that here:

www.SurvivalFitnessPlan.com/Essential-Parkour-Review-Amazon

Claim your bonus materials:

www.SurvivalFitnessPlan.com/Book-Bonuses

Connect with like-minded people and discuss anything SFP related via the SFP Facebook group:

www.Facebook.com/groups/SurvivalFitnessPlan

A list of resources used in the creation of the Survival Fitness Series is available at:

www.SurvivalFitnessPlan.com/Survival-Fitness-Series

Thanks again for your support,

Sam Fury, Author.

AUTHOR RECOMMENDATIONS

This is Your Ultimate Fitness Program

This is the last fitness manual you'll ever need, because it is functional training at it's best!

Get it now.

www.SurvivalFitnessPlan.com/Survival-Fitness

Teach Yourself Escape and Evasion Tactics!

Discover the skills you need to evade and escape capture, because you never know when they will save your life!

Get it now.

www.SurvivalFitnessPlan.com/Evading-Escaping-Capture

SURVIVAL FITNESS PLAN TRAINING MANUALS

Survival Fitness

When in danger, you have two options: fight or flight.

This series contains training manuals on the best methods of flight. Together with self-defense, you can train in them for general health and fitness.

- **Parkour.** All the parkour skills you need to overcome obstacles in your path.
- **Climbing.** Focusing on essential bouldering techniques.
- **Riding.** Essential mountain-bike riding techniques. Go as fast as possible in the safest manner.
- **Swimming.** Swimming for endurance and/or speed using the most efficient strokes.

It also has books covering general health and wellness, such as yoga and meditation.

www.SurvivalFitnessPlan.com/Survival-Fitness-Series

Self-Defense

The Self-Defense Series has volumes on some of the martial arts used as a base in SFP self-defense.

It also contains the SFP self-defense training manuals. SFP Self-Defense is an efficient and effective form of minimalist self-defense.

www.SurvivalFitnessPlan.com/Self-Defense-Series

Escape, Evasion, and Survival

SFP escape, evasion, and survival (EES) focuses on keeping you alive using minimal resources. Subjects covered include:

- **Disaster Survival.** How to prepare for and react in the case of disaster and/or societal collapse.
- **Escape and Evasion.** The ability to escape capture and hide from your enemy.
- **Urban and Wilderness Survival.** Being able to live off the land in all terrains.
- **Emergency Roping.** Basic climbing skills and improvised roping techniques.
- **Water Rescue.** Life-saving water skills based on surf life-saving and military training course competencies.
- **Wilderness First Aid.** Modern medicine for use in emergency situations.

www.SurvivalFitnessPlan.com/Escape-Evasion-Survival-Series

Sustainable Living

Create a lifestyle focused on minimal impact to the environment and maximum self-reliance.

SFP sustainable living subjects include permaculture, renewable energy, financial freedom, minimalist living, and more.

www.SurvivalFitnessPlan.com/Sustainable-Living-Series

Miscellaneous

Books by the SFP authors that do not fit into any of the major series.

www.SurvivalFitnessPlan.com/Miscellaneous-Titles

ABOUT THE AUTHOR

Sam Fury has had a passion for survival, evasion, resistance, and escape (SERE) training since he was a young boy growing up in Australia.

This led him to years of training and career experience in related subjects, including martial arts, military training, survival skills, outdoor sports, and sustainable living.

These days, Sam spends his time refining existing skills, gaining new skills, and sharing what he learns via the Survival Fitness Plan website.

www.SurvivalFitnessPlan.com

amazon.com/author/samfury

facebook.com/SurvivalFitnessPlan

twitter.com/Survival_Fitnes

pinterest.com/survivalfitnes

goodreads.com/SamFury

bookbub.com/authors/sam-fury

Printed in Great Britain
by Amazon